HARD NUTS
OF HISTORY
Kings and
Queens

TRACEY TURNER

ILLUSTRATED BY JAMIE LENMAN

A & C BLACK
AN IMPRINT OF BLOOMSBURY
LONDON NEW DELHI NEW YORK SYDNEY

First published 2015 by

A & C Black, an imprint of Bloomsbury Publishing Plc

50 Bedford Square, London WC1B 3DP

www.bloomsbury.com

Bloomsbury is a registered trademark of Bloomsbury Publishing Plc

ISBN 978-1-4729-1092-9

A CIP catalogue for this book is available from the British Library.

This book is produced using paper that is made from wood grown in managed,
sustainable forests. It is natural, renewable and recyclable. The logging and
manufacturing processes conform to the environmental regulations of the country
of origin.

Printed in China by Leo Paper Products, Heshan, Guangdong

1 3 5 7 9 10 8 6 4 2

CONTENTS

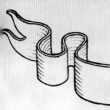

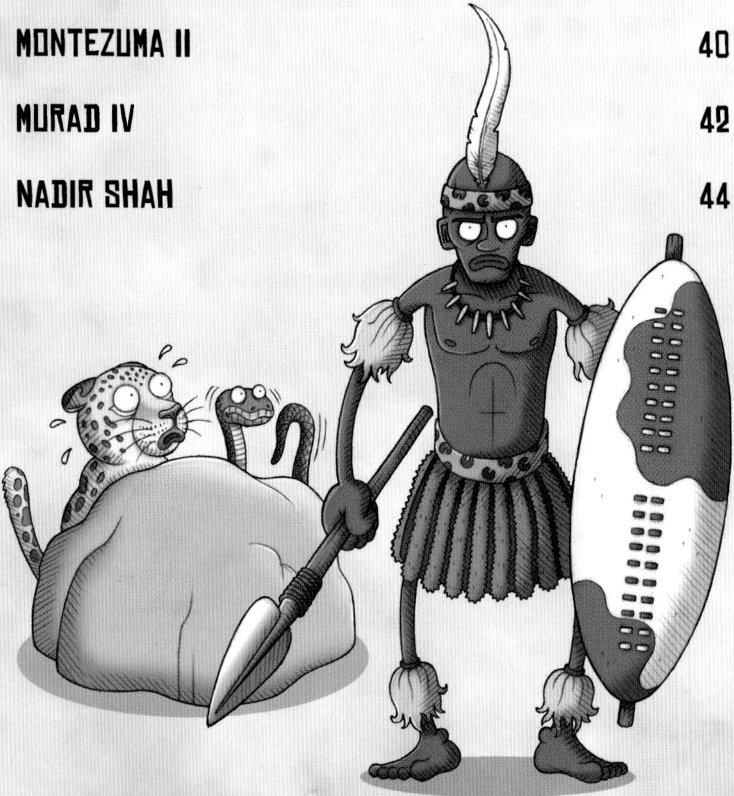

INTRODUCTION

This book contains some of the hardest kings and queens ever, from terrifying tsars to savage sultans. Some of them were power-crazed tyrants, some were axe-wielding warriors, and some were very strange indeed. But all of them were as hard as nails.

FIND OUT ABOUT . . .

• Horrible human sacrifice

• Brave runaway slaves

• Tremendous elephant-mounted armies

• Head-chopping, eye-gouging and burning at the stake

If you've ever wanted to be worshipped by millions, command a Persian fleet, or become Empress of China, read on. Follow the hard nuts through the plains of central India, into the Aztec capital city, and across the Pacific Ocean by canoe.

As well as discovering stories of courage and cunning, you might be in for a few surprises. Did you know that King Henry VIII had more than 50,000 heads chopped off? Or that Thutmose III tried to have his predecessor's name deleted from history.

You're about to meet some of the toughest kings and queens in history . . .

Plus take the quiz on page 28 and find out how well you know your monarch nicknames!

QUEEN ARTEMISIA OF HALICARNASSUS

Queen Artemisia was a brave and clever sea commander in the Persian War with Greece.

PERSIAN OVERLORDS

Artemisia was Queen of Halicarnassus, which was part of the massive and mighty Persian Empire. Artemisia was tough, but she wasn't stupid: she was a fierce warrior queen and she nearly changed the course of history.

COUNCIL OF WAR

The powerful Persian Emperor Xerxes I, was very keen on expanding his empire into Greece and had already made one unsuccessful attempt at grabbing Greece before he turned to Artemisia and the other commanders of the Persian fleet in 480 BC. Artemisia was unusual among the Persian commanders in two ways: first, she was a woman. Second, she was the only commander who advised Xerxes against his planned sea battle. She thought it was too risky, and would be better to wait. Xerxes listened and praised Artemisia for her wise advice. Then he completely ignored it and gave the order to set sail.

HARDOMETER

CUNNING: 8
COURAGE: 9
SURVIVAL SKILLS: 8
RUTHLESSNESS: 8

THE BATTLE OF SALAMIS

Artemisia was in command of five ships at the Battle of Salamis. She fought bravely and with ruthless cunning, sometimes flying the Greek flag to confuse her enemies.

At one point in the battle her ship became trapped, with a Persian ship blocking her escape route – so she rammed the ship and sank it in order to get away. Xerxes didn't seem to mind, though. He thought Artemisia was his best commander and it is reported he said, "My men have become women and my women men," (which was the way a lot of people thought in those days). However, despite Artemisia's best efforts, the Persians were completely trounced.

PERSIANS GO HOME

Xerxes consulted his commanders on whether he should leave some of the Persian fleet in Greece, and this time he listened to Artemisia: they all went home. If he'd taken her advice in the first place, maybe the Persians would have conquered Greece and changed the course of history. The Greeks, meanwhile, were very happy they'd won, but absolutely furious that a woman had commanded ships in a battle against their fleet. They offered a reward for her capture, but no one ever succeeded.

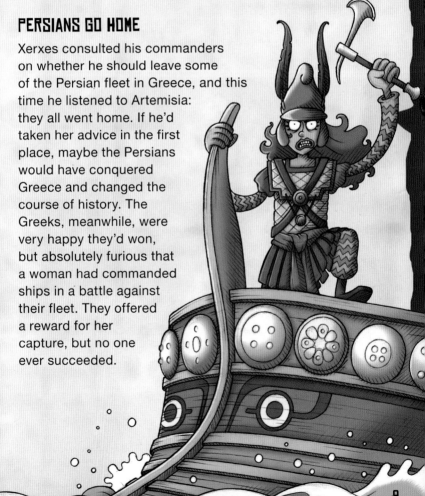

HENRY VIII OF ENGLAND

HARD NUT RATING: 7.3

Henry VIII is probably the best-known English king – famous for having six wives and plenty of head-chopping.

HANDSOME HENRY

Henry wasn't supposed to be king at all, but became heir when his older brother died. He was a tall, strapping 18-year-old when he became king in 1509. He was clever, musical, good at horse-riding and archery, and very popular, despite the expensive war against France. (To keep the French at bay, Henry increased the size of the navy ten times, including adding the world's biggest ship.)

UPSETTING THE POPE

Henry was married to the Spanish princess Catherine of Aragon for nearly 24 years. They had a daughter, but Henry desperately wanted a son who'd become king after him. So he divorced Catherine and married Anne Boleyn, and as a result the Pope chucked him out of the Catholic Church, because divorce wasn't allowed. Henry set up the Church of England, with himself as its head. This gave him a great excuse to get rid of 800 monasteries and sell off their land and wealth.

SEVERAL MORE WIVES

Anne Boleyn was the second of Henry's six wives. He had her beheaded, and the same fate was in store for his fifth wife, Catherine Howard. In between there was Jane Seymour, who died soon after producing a son for Henry, and Anne of Cleves, who Henry divorced because he thought she wasn't as nice-looking as the portrait he'd seen of her before they met. Henry's sixth wife, Catherine Parr, outlived him.

OFF WITH HIS HEAD!

Wives weren't the only people Henry had executed. Henry set a record for beheadings. No one's quite sure how many people were executed during Henry's reign, but it's probably somewhere between 57,000 and 72,000. Henry became more and more ruthless, and had a growing habit of executing men who'd once been close friends and advisors.

AFTER HENRY

In his last years Henry became very fat and unwell, with painful ulcers on his legs that made it difficult for him to move about. He died in 1547, and his nine-year-old son became Edward VI, but he died six years later. Both Henry's daughters, Mary and Elizabeth (see page 46) became queen after that.

HARDOMETER

CUNNING: 8
COURAGE: 6
SURVIVAL SKILLS: 5
RUTHLESSNESS: 10

FERDINAND II AND ISABELLA I OF SPAIN

Ferdinand and Isabella were the first king and queen of a united Spain, and were known as the Catholic Monarchs because they were so keen on their religion.

UNITED SPAIN

Isabella was Queen of Castile when she married Ferdinand, the King of Aragon, uniting the two big Spanish kingdoms, though they carried on being ruled separately at first. Before the end of their reign, the whole of Spain would be united.

KEEN CHRISTIANS

Ferdinand and Isabella were Catholics, and they were fed up with people from other religions starting rebellions. So they chucked all the Jewish and Muslim people out of Spain, apart from anyone who converted to Christianity. But then they began to accuse those who had converted to Christianity of going back to their old religion, and imprisoned, interrogated, tortured and even burned to death hundreds of them.

HARDOMETER

CUNNING: 7
COURAGE: 6
SURVIVAL SKILLS: 9
RUTHLESSNESS: 9

GRABBING GRANADA

The Catholic Monarchs were very annoyed that a large chunk of Spain was ruled by Muslims – invaders from North Africa, known as Moors, who'd ruled most of Spain for hundreds of years. By the time Ferdinand and Isabella were in charge, the Moors still ruled the Kingdom of Granada. But Ferdinand and Isabella were about to put a stop to that: after ten years of fighting, the Moors were finally defeated at the city of Granada in 1492.

NEW WORLD RICHES

Once they'd got rid of the Moors and the other non-Christians, Ferdinand and Isabella could concentrate on other things – like discovering the New World. In 1492 they funded Christopher Columbus's expedition to find a sea route to India by sailing west. The new lands he discovered were claimed for Spain (without asking the people who already lived there), and Spain became richer as a result.

MARRIAGES AND AGREEMENTS

Ferdinand and Isabella were keen to protect their united country. They signed agreements with England and the Holy Roman Empire, and married some of their children off to royal families who supported them in the rest of Europe (including Catherine of Aragon, who married Henry VIII – see page 10). Isabella died in 1504, and Ferdinand 12 years later. Spain has stayed united ever since.

13

ASHURNASIRPAL II OF ASSYRIA

Ashurnasirpal was a conquering king who made Assyria wealthy and powerful.

HARD TIMES

Ashurnasirpal became king of Assyria (now part of Iraq) in 883 BC. Assyria had been a powerful country in the past, but by Ashurnasirpal's time things weren't going so well, and the country had lost some of its land. Ashurnasirpal had plans to make Assyria – and himself – much richer and more powerful.

CRUEL CONQUEROR

Ashurnasirpal marched his army to the north and east of Assyria in a series of attacks against neighbouring lands, and made local rulers send him money and gifts, and accept him as their ruler. He was utterly ruthless if anyone opposed him. He had governors publically whipped, burned many of the prisoners he captured, blinded enemy soldiers or cut off their hands, noses or ears. At least, according to his own inscriptions in his new capital city – he liked to boast.

CAPITAL CITY

Ashurnasirpal used the loot and the prisoners of war to build an extremely impressive new capital city at Kalhu (modern-day Nimrud in Iraq). Kalhu included a luxurious palace and zoological and botanical gardens. Canals were built from the Great Zab River to water them. The palace was huge. An inscription at the palace mentions a banquet for 69,574 guests lasting ten days to celebrate the opening

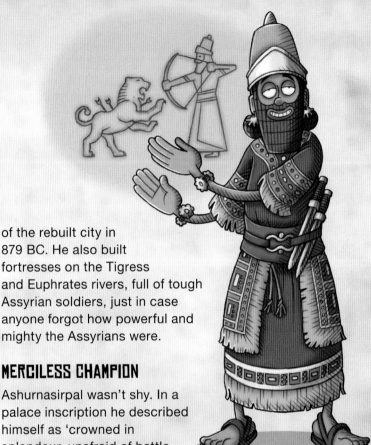

of the rebuilt city in 879 BC. He also built fortresses on the Tigress and Euphrates rivers, full of tough Assyrian soldiers, just in case anyone forgot how powerful and mighty the Assyrians were.

MERCILESS CHAMPION

Ashurnasirpal wasn't shy. In a palace inscription he described himself as 'crowned in splendour, unafraid of battle, the merciless champion who shakes resistance, the glorious king, the shepherd, the protector of the whole world . . .' He also claimed to have personally killed 450 lions. When Ashurnasirpal died in 859 BC, he'd conquered most of the land that had been lost centuries before, and established a new Assyrian Empire, in the 24 years he'd been king.

HARDOMETER

CUNNING: 8
COURAGE: 6
SURVIVAL SKILLS: 8
RUTHLESSNESS: 10

ANCIENT EMPIRES

Most of us have heard of the Ancient Greeks and Romans. But thousands of years before them, cities were built, civilisations flourished, and empires were created . . .

MESOPOTAMIA

The world's first cities were built in Sumer, southern Mesopotamia (modern-day Iraq), in the fertile land between the Tigris and Euphrates Rivers. Uruk, considered the world's first city, was built around 6,500 years ago. Different empires came and went in Mesopotamia:

- Sargon, the world's first emperor, ruled the Akkadian Empire in Sumer in around 2300 BC.

- Babylonia had the world's first written laws – its capital, Babylon, was built around 1900 BC and later had famous gardens.

- The fierce Hittites, who came from what's now southern Turkey, bashed the Babylonians and destroyed Babylon . . .

- . . . then the Assyrians, expert charioteers, conquered the Hittites in the eighth century BC.

- The Babylonians (called the New Babylonians by historians to avoid confusion) defeated the Assyrians in 608 BC. They could predict eclipses of the moon.

- Finally the Persian Empire, started by hard nut King Cyrus, covered all the land of the earlier Mesopotamian empires – the biggest empire in the world up to that time.

ANCIENT EGYPT

Egypt was the world's first country. Upper and Lower Egypt were united by King Narmer around 3200 BC. It lasted for almost 3,000 years, until it became part of Alexander the Great's empire in 332 BC. After that it was ruled by non-Egyptian pharaohs (the first one was Alexander the Great's general, Ptolemy).

ANCIENT CHINA

The first cities were built in the Yellow River valley in China around 1600 BC. The first Chinese emperor, Shihuangdi, united the different states of China in 206 BC. After Shihuangdi's Qin dynasty, China was ruled by a series of dynasties until the 20th century.

ANCIENT INDIA

The first civilisation in the Indus Valley is mysterious – it was only discovered 150 years ago, and no one knows much about it. Cities, such as Mohenjo-Daro, were built more than 4,000 years ago, with roads, sewers, and even toilets, but no huge palaces or temples. Its written language is still waiting to be deciphered.

HARALD HARDRADA

Viking King Harald's nickname, Hardrada, means 'hard ruler', and it's not difficult to see how he got it.

HARD NUT
RATING: 7

FIERCE FIGHTER

Harald's brother tried to get his hands on the Danish throne and so Harald fought in his first big battle in 1030, when he was 15, against the Danish King Cnut. Harald was wounded and lost the battle, but it didn't put him off fighting. He joined the army of Yaroslav the Wise in Russia, moved on to Constantinople, where he commanded a tough, axe-wielding unit of the Byzantine Army, and grew very rich at the same time.

KING OF NORWAY

Harald left Constantinople because he had his eye on the throne of Norway, which was occupied by his nephew, Magnus the Good. Harald persuaded Magnus to become joint king with him, and share Harald's massive wealth. Conveniently, Magnus died the following year. To make sure he stayed king, Harald crushed opposition to his rule and had political opponents assassinated. Next he began making raids on the Danish coast and fought the Danish King, in an attempt to become King of Denmark too, but in the end he gave up.

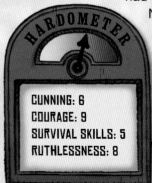

HARDOMETER

CUNNING: 6
COURAGE: 9
SURVIVAL SKILLS: 5
RUTHLESSNESS: 8

HARALD VS HAROLD

The King of England was Harold Godwinson. Godwinson's brother, Tostig, suggested to Harald Hardrada that he might want to become the King of England instead, with Tostig's help – after a revolt, Harald had taken Tostig's title of Earl of Northumbria instead of sticking up for his brother. Harald didn't need asking twice: he landed on the coast of northern England in 1066 with 300 ships, and defeated English troops at the Battle of Fulford. He captured York, and things seemed to be going well.

THE BATTLE OF STAMFORD BRIDGE

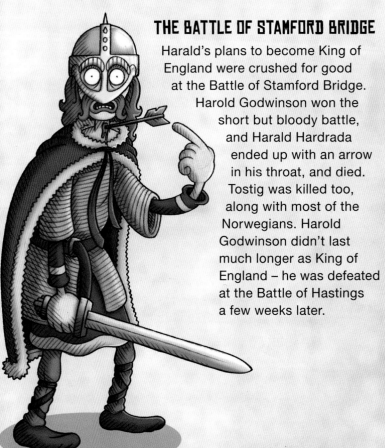

Harald's plans to become King of England were crushed for good at the Battle of Stamford Bridge. Harold Godwinson won the short but bloody battle, and Harald Hardrada ended up with an arrow in his throat, and died. Tostig was killed too, along with most of the Norwegians. Harold Godwinson didn't last much longer as King of England – he was defeated at the Battle of Hastings a few weeks later.

NZINGA MBANDE

Nzinga Mbande was an African queen who set up an army camp for runaway slaves and successfully defended her kingdom.

HARD NUT
RATING: 7.5

PORTUGUESE INVADERS

At the beginning of the 1600s, African states on the Central African coast were threatened by the Portuguese. They wanted to take charge of the region and control the trade of African slaves, who were shipped across the Atlantic to the New World. The Portuguese governor of Luanda (today the capital of Angola), went to war with the Kingdom of Ndongo. King Ngola Mbandi of the Ndongo ran away, and thousands of Ndongo people became prisoners of the Portuguese, leaving Ngola's tough sister, Nzinga, to sort things out.

NZINGA IN CHARGE

There are lots of different versions of Nzinga's story – some say that her brother killed himself, while others say that Nzinga killed him so that she could seize power. But whatever happened, Nzinga ended up in charge in 1624. She agreed with the Portuguese that they should return the Ndongo prisoners, and remove the fortress they'd built on Ndongo land, but within a couple of years she'd been betrayed.

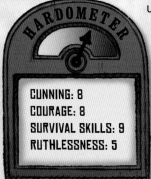

HARDOMETER

CUNNING: 8
COURAGE: 8
SURVIVAL SKILLS: 9
RUTHLESSNESS: 5

LEAVING NDONGO

Nzinga and her people fled further west, and founded a new state at Matamba. Nzinga set up a military school, and invited runaway slaves and African soldiers trained by the Portuguese to join. She also stirred up trouble in Ndongo, which was now controlled by the Portuguese.

DUTCH FRIENDS

The Dutch also wanted to get rid of the Portuguese, and Nzinga became their ally. At one point, the Dutch captured Luanda, but even with Nzinga's help they couldn't drive out the Portuguese completely, and Luanda was recaptured. Nzinga retreated to Matamba again, and focused on looking after her land, protecting it from the Portuguese, and making it rich. She was still fighting against the Portuguese into her sixties.

OLD ENEMIES

Nzinga achieved her aims, and by the time she died of old age when she was 81 she'd gained the respect of her old enemies. Her kingdom of Matamba was able to trade on an equal footing with the Europeans.

CHANDRAGUPTA

Chandragupta conquered vast chunks of India, and began the massive Mauryan Empire.

HARD NUT
RATING: 6.3

DISUNITED INDIA

When Chandragupta was born in 340 BC, India wasn't a united country but was made up of lots of different independent states. The biggest was the Magadha Kingdom in northern India, ruled by the Nanda Dynasty. Another large chunk of northern India had been defeated by Alexander the Great in 326 BC and became part of the Macedonian Empire.

THROWING OUT THE NANDAS

Chandragupta was related to the Nandas but lived in exile. He decided to boot out the Macedonians and the Nanda Dynasty, and make a new empire himself. With his cunning advisor, Kautilya Chanakya, he raised an army, marched on the Nanda capital, Pataliputra, and started a civil war. In 322 BC he grabbed the throne and threw out the Nandas for good, and began his own Mauryan Dynasty.

NORTHERN CONQUERING

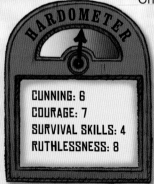

HARDOMETER

CUNNING: 6
COURAGE: 7
SURVIVAL SKILLS: 4
RUTHLESSNESS: 8

Chandragupta expanded his territory by attacking the Macedonian General Seleucus and grabbing some of modern-day Pakistan and Afghanistan. Eventually, Chandragupta and Seleucus agreed the borders of their neighbouring territories, and Chandragupta gained the Punjab in northern India in return for 500 war elephants.

SOUTHERN CONQUERING

Chandragupta ruled from his vast capital city at Pataliputra, and kept an army of 60,000 foot soldiers, 30,000 cavalry and 9,000 war elephants. Now that he had most of northern India (and quite a bit more besides) in his clutches, he marched his army south, and succeeded in conquering more land. He ended up with most of northern and central India, though he was rather annoyed that the Kingdom of Kalinga remained out of his empire in the east.

ENORMOUS EMPIRE

Chandragupta gave up being emperor in 298 BC, and passed the government of his Mauryan Empire on to his son. His grandson, Ashoka, expanded the empire to its largest extent: it covered almost the whole of India, and a lot of what is now Pakistan, Afghanistan and Bangladesh, and lasted until 185 BC. Chandragupta became a follower of the non-violent Jain religion, and is said to have starved himself to death in a cave.

KING KAMEHAMEHA I

King Kamehameha was a fierce warrior king who united and ruled the Hawaiian Islands.

HARD NUT
RATING: 8

YOUNG KAMEHAMEHA

When Kamehameha was born around 1758, legend has it that storms and strange lights in the sky were signs that he would become a great chief. He was trained to fight and navigate, the two most important skills for a hard nut Hawaiian chief. When he was 14, he overturned the Naha Stone (or so the story goes) – a massive great rock that weighs up to 3.5 tonnes. It was said that whoever could lift the stone would unite the Hawaiian Islands.

HAWAIIAN FIGHTING

There was an awful lot of fighting in the Hawaiian Islands – when a king died it almost always meant a huge punch-up over who would take control. When Captain Cook arrived in 1779, some Hawaiians thought he was Lono, the god of peace and plenty. So fighting stopped for a while, but once they'd realised Cook wasn't a god, just an English explorer, fighting resumed. By this time, Kamehameha had proved himself a tough warrior, and was at the battle in which Captain Cook was killed.

KING OF HAWAII

Kamehameha's cousin became King of Hawaii when Kamehameha's uncle died in 1782. The two cousins didn't get on. Five chiefs supported Kamehameha, and, after several fights, his cousin was eventually defeated and killed. Kamehameha still had to convince the other Hawaiian chiefs to support him, but in 1791, he became King of Hawaii, having bashed everyone else into submission.

UNITED ISLANDS

Over the next 19 years, Kamehameha fought all the other islands, with his fleets of canoes and 10,000 soldiers. He was a ferocious warrior, but he was given a helping hand by new European weapons – his warriors now had muskets and cannons. Eventually, after a lot of fighting, Kamehameha became ruler of all the Hawaiian Islands in 1810.

INDEPENDENT HAWAII

Kamehameha managed his united Hawaiian Islands skilfully, dealing with Americans, English, Spanish and Russians, who all wanted the islands for themselves. He encouraged trade, but kept Hawaii independent. Kamehameha died in 1819. Hawaii was finally made part of the United States of America in 1898.

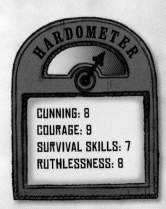

HARDOMETER

CUNNING: 8
COURAGE: 9
SURVIVAL SKILLS: 7
RUTHLESSNESS: 8

HATSHEPSUT

Hatshepsut changed the way ancient Egypt was run, and became its first female ruler.

HARD NUT
RATING: 8.8

PHANTASTIC PHARAOHS

Pharaohs were powerful kings who ruled Egypt from around 5,000 years ago until 30 BC, when Cleopatra died. Hatshepsut lived around 3,500 years ago, the daughter of the warrior pharaoh Thutmose I, and his wife Ahmose. She became the chief wife of Thutmose II, who was also Thutmose I's son and Hatshepsut's half-brother (the Egyptian royal families often married their own brothers and sisters because it strengthened their claim to the throne). When Hatshepsut's husband/brother died in about 1479 BC, Hatshepsut didn't have any sons, so Thutmose's son by a different wife became the new pharaoh, Thutmose III.

BECOMING PHARAOH

Thutmose was still a child, so Hatshepsut ruled for him, supposedly until he was old enough to rule on his own. But, after a few years, Hatshepsut decided she liked being the most important person in the known world, and made sure it stayed that way by having herself crowned pharaoh. This was the first time a woman had ever become pharaoh of Egypt. Even when Thutmose had grown up, Hatshepsut ruled alongside him. Pharaohs were worshipped as gods, and when they died they were believed to take their place among the other Egyptian gods – and hard nut Hatshepsut did not want to give that up.

WAR AND PEACE

Hatshepsut's reign was peaceful – though she might have taken part in a battle against Nubia, to the south of ancient Egypt. Instead of fighting, she travelled to the land of Punt, which is believed to be in north eastern Africa, and brought back exotic spices and plants, gold and ebony. She also built impressive and expensive buildings, including her temple at Deir el-Bahri.

REWRITING THE PAST

Hatshepsut died in 1458 BC and Thutmose III could finally rule on his own. Towards the end of his reign, Thutmose removed Hatshepsut's name from temples and inscriptions, maybe in an attempt to make his own name go down in history as Egypt's greatest ruler, or maybe because he wanted his revenge. Either way, he didn't succeed, and Hatshepsut is still remembered as the first female Egyptian pharaoh.

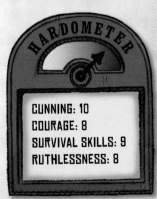

HARDOMETER

CUNNING: 10
COURAGE: 8
SURVIVAL SKILLS: 9
RUTHLESSNESS: 8

NAME THAT MONARCH!

Like Suleiman the Magnificent (page 50) and Frederick the Great (page 34), some kings and queens have been given names that make them sound impressive. Others have nicknames that don't sound so tough. Can you give these monarchs the right names?

1. Ordono the Wicked ruled Leon in Spain from 958 to 960, taking over from Sancho the . . .

a) Ugly

b) Skinny

c) Fat

2. Polish ruler Boleslaw IV was nicknamed Boleslaw the . . .

a) Curly

b) Hairy

c) Bald

SULEIMAN THE MAGNIFICENT

3. Legendary Viking ruler Ragnar Lodbrok's name translates as . . .

a) Bushy Beard

b) Twirly Moustache

c) Hairy Trousers

4. Uros V of Serbia was known as Uros the . . .

a) Timid

b) Weak

c) Strong

5. Peter I of Portugal was known as Peter the . . .

a) Bad-tempered

b) Cruel

c) Hot-head

6. Spanish Queen Joanna the Mad was married to Philip the . . .

a) Sane

b) Handsome

c) Stupid

7. Bulgarian Tsar Ivaylo was known as the . . .

a) Turnip

b) Cabbage

c) Carrot

8. Olaf III of Norway was Olaf the . . .

a) Loud

b) Proud

c) Quiet

9. Charlemagne, warrior king of the Franks, had a father known as Pippin the . . .

a) Pint-sized

b) Tall

c) Short

10. Charles VI of France was nicknamed Charles the . . .

a) Mad

b) Sad

c) Bad

KING SHAKA

Shaka was a hard nut Zulu king who did a lot of fighting and a lot of conquering.

HARD NUT
RATING: 8

SNAKES AND LEOPARDS

Shaka was born around 1787, the son of a Zulu chief, but because his parents weren't married, he wasn't next in line to become chief when his father died. He grew up tough: according to legend, when he was 13 he killed a deadly black mamba snake, and when he was 19 he killed an attacking leopard. Shaka became a warrior under chieftain Dingiswayo, chief of the Mthethwa, who were in charge of the Zulu. Shaka was such a fierce warrior that Dingiswayo made him commander of his unit.

MURDER AND REVENGE

When Shaka's father died, Shaka's younger brother became chief of the Zulus. But not for long: Shaka had him assassinated, and became chief instead – though Dingiswayo was still in overall charge. When Dingiswayo was murdered by a chief called Zwide, Shaka promised revenge. Zwide escaped his clutches, so Shaka took his revenge on Zwide's mother by burning down her house. Zwide and Shaka continued to be deadly enemies and around 1825, the two chiefs met in battle, and Zwide was defeated.

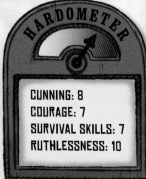

CUNNING: 8
COURAGE: 7
SURVIVAL SKILLS: 7
RUTHLESSNESS: 10

CONQUERING

Shaka expanded his lands, either by conquering other tribes or by persuading them that they were better off united, with Shaka in charge. His success was partly due to clever new battle tactics and weapons, including a short sword instead of a throwing spear. But he made plenty of enemies too, especially after his mother died, when he started behaving very oddly . . .

MAKING ENEMIES

Shaka ordered that no crops should be planted and no milk used during the mourning period for his mother. He had thousands of people executed because he thought they weren't grief-stricken enough, and killed cows so that their calves would experience losing their mothers. Among Shaka's enemies were two of his half-brothers, Dingane and Mhlangana. They'd probably tried to kill him a couple of times before they finally managed it, in 1828.

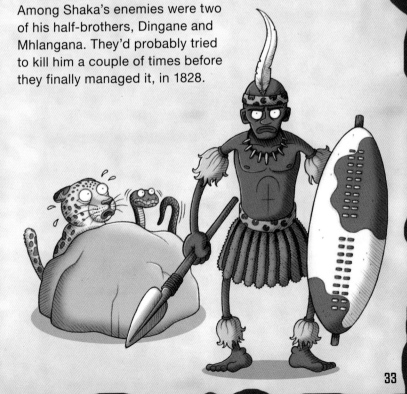

FREDERICK THE GREAT

HARD NUT RATING: 7.5

Frederick the Great did lots of conquering, and made Prussia the most powerful country in Europe.

A BAD BEGINNING

Frederick was born in Berlin, the son of King William I of Prussia (a country that doesn't exist now but included parts of present-day Germany and surrounding countries). Things didn't begin well for Frederick: his father wanted him to be a hard nut soldier, but Frederick liked music, art, and studying, and they got on so badly that William had his son beaten in public. When he was 18 Frederick ran away, but was captured and his best friend, who'd gone with him, was executed.

WAR WITH AUSTRIA

Frederick became King of Prussia in 1740, when he was 28. In the end, his father would have been pleased: Frederick did become a hard nut soldier. One of the first things he did as King was to use his father's large and well-trained army to invade Silesia, a rich Austrian Province (which is now part of Poland). This was the start of years of war with Austria, which tried and failed to recapture Silesia. Finally, Austria joined up with some powerful friends, France, Russia, Sweden and Saxony.

THE SEVEN YEARS' WAR

Frederick had England on his side, so more or less the whole of Europe was now at war – and it was all Frederick's fault. He conquered Saxony, invaded Bohemia (which is now part of the Czech Republic), and won battles against the

Austrians, the French and the Swedes. Finally, in 1763, the alliances fell apart, and Austria made peace with Prussia. Around 180,000 Prussian troops died in the Seven Years' War. After all that fighting, Frederick still hung on to Silesia.

CONQUERING

Frederick managed to almost double the size of Prussia in the end, partly through making agreements with other countries but mostly by invading at the head of a very large army. Everyone in Prussia had to fight – in fact Frederick had to call in foreign troops, and raise huge taxes to pay them. Frederick died in 1786, having reigned for 46 years. Prussia was now much bigger and more powerful than it had been when he became king.

HARDOMETER

CUNNING: 7
COURAGE: 7
SURVIVAL SKILLS: 8
RUTHLESSNESS: 8

QUEEN ZENOBIA

Zenobia was a conquering queen who created an empire and rebelled against the ancient Romans.

HARD NUT
RATING: 8.8

QUEEN ZENOBIA

Zenobia was Queen of Palmyra, in what's now Syria. Her husband was made governor of the area by the Romans but he and Zenobia's step-son were both assassinated in 267 AD. There were stories that Zenobia had them both killed so that she could grab power for herself. Zenobia's baby son Vaballathus was made King, with Zenobia ruling for him.

TROUBLE WITH THE SASSANIDS

Palmyra was next to the Sassanid Empire, based in what's now Iran. The Sassanids were some of the many people causing trouble for the Romans, as their empire expanded into Roman territory. Zenobia led her troops against them and won, gaining more land for Palmyra.

INVASIONS

Zenobia's husband had been happy to rule Palmyra as part of the Roman Empire. But Zenobia wasn't. She led her army in an attack against Egypt. She won, and proclaimed herself Queen of Egypt. Then she began a path of destruction across Anatolia (in what's now Turkey), Syria, Palestine and Lebanon, conquering as she went. She declared herself independent from the Roman Empire, the ruler of her own Palmyrene Empire.

DEFEAT

Bits had started to drop off the Roman Empire by Zenobia's time: it had split into two halves, and was weaker than it had been, and faced attack along some of its borders. But the Roman Emperor Aurelian wasn't about to lose another chunk of his empire. His army defeated Zenobia in battle, then besieged the city of Palmyra.

CAPTURED

Zenobia and her son Vaballathus tried to escape, but were soon captured. The Palmyrenes were forced to surrender (and anyone who didn't was executed), and Zenobia and Vaballathus were taken to Rome. What happened to them in the end is a mystery: Zenobia might have killed herself on the way to Rome, or been executed once she got there. There's one story that the emperor took pity on her, and allowed her to live the rest of her life in a comfortable villa in Italy.

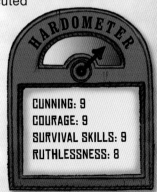

HARDOMETER

CUNNING: 9
COURAGE: 9
SURVIVAL SKILLS: 9
RUTHLESSNESS: 8

WARRIOR KINGS AND QUEENS

Some kings and queens, like Ferdinand and
Isabella of Spain, sent their armies to war to fight
for them. But others, like Queen Zenobia and
Harald Hardrada, were tougher, and liked to get
involved themselves. Here are some more of the
hardest warrior kings and queens of all time.

QUEEN BOUDICA

Possibly the most famous warrior queen of all, Boudica
was Queen of the British Iceni tribe in the first century. She
stood up to the ancient Romans, defeated Roman troops
and ransacked their capital. She was finally beaten in a
battle with the Roman governor of Britain, Suetonius. She
killed herself rather than face capture.

WILLIAM THE CONQUEROR

William was the tough nut Norman duke who invaded
England in 1066, defeated King Harold at the Battle of
Hastings, and made himself King of England. He did a lot
of marauding, burning, and generally making himself very
unpopular with the natives, but he ruled for more than 20
years and passed the crown on to his son.

CHARLEMAGNE

Charlemagne was King of the Franks in the Middle Ages on
a mission to convert everyone to Christianity and conquer
as many places as possible while he was doing it. He
ruthlessly executed 4,500 Saxons in one go. He conquered
lots of Europe and founded an empire that would last nearly
1,000 years.

ATTILA THE HUN

Attila, King of the Huns, led some of the most feared warriors in Europe in the 400s AD. He led his rampaging Huns on a path of destruction across the eastern and western halves of the Roman Empire, demanding gold, destroying cities, and setting fire to things.

ERIC BLOODAXE

Viking warrior King Eric Bloodaxe murdered his brothers so that he would become King of Norway. When Bloodaxe was driven out by a surviving brother, he set sail for the British Isles, raided Scotland, and became King of Northumbria.

QUEEN JUDITH

Judith became queen of a Jewish Kingdom in Ethiopia in the 900s. She's supposed to have killed the emperor and put herself in charge, and during her 40-year reign she tried to wipe out all the members of the old ruling family, destroying anything or anyone that stood in her way.

MONTEZUMA II

Montezuma was a conquering Aztec Emperor and a great warrior, but didn't last long after the invading Spanish arrived.

HARD NUT
RATING: 7.5

AZTEC CONQUERORS

Montezuma was born around 1466 in Tenochtitlan, the beautiful capital city of the Aztecs that's now Mexico City. The Aztec Empire controlled a lot of Central America and all of what's now Mexico, and ruled five to six million people. Montezuma became a famously fearsome warrior, and helped conquer more land for the Aztecs.

AZTEC EMPEROR

In 1502, Montezuma became Aztec Emperor. The same year he crushed a rebellion, so he used captives from the battle as human sacrifices at his coronation. The Aztecs made a lot of human sacrifices to their gods, and demanded sacrifice victims from the people they'd conquered. This was probably why Montezuma had to deal with quite a lot of rebellions while he was emperor. When he wasn't dealing with those, he was conquering, and the Aztec Empire reached its largest size under Montezuma's rule.

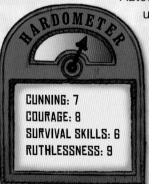

HARDOMETER

CUNNING: 7
COURAGE: 8
SURVIVAL SKILLS: 6
RUTHLESSNESS: 9

GOOD GOD!

Mexico had recently been discovered by Europeans. The Spanish conqueror, Hernàn Cortés, who'd already done a bit of conquering in Cuba, wanted to get his hands on the rich Aztec Empire. He contacted some of the many people who were fed up with being ruled by the Aztecs, and ended up with 1,000 warriors on his side from the Tlaxcaltec tribe, as well as his own troops. The story goes that Montezuma welcomed Cortés into his capital city, thinking he was the god Quetzalcoatl (a prophesy said he would be white-skinned and have a beard). Cortés wasn't so trusting: he assumed the welcome was a trap, and took Montezuma hostage.

MONTEZUMA'S END

Cortés had to leave Tenochtitlan for a punch-up with a Spanish enemy, and while he was away the Aztecs rebelled. By the time Cortés got back, the Spanish had been driven out of the Aztec capital, and Montezuma had been killed in the fighting. Spanish accounts say that Montezuma was killed by the Aztecs, who threw stones at him when the Spanish showed him to his people. Aztec accounts say that he was killed by the Spanish. After his death, in 1520, Montezuma's empire fell to the Spanish.

MURAD IV

Murad was a fearsome Ottoman Sultan who conquered Baghdad and executed anyone who opposed him.

HARD NUT
RATING: 7.8

BARMY ARMY

When Murad was born, in 1612, the Ottoman Empire was already more than 300 years old. Murad was just 11 when he became Sultan, and his mother and various viziers ruled for him for a few years because he was too young. However, the cavalry and army were really in control, and executed officials without his consent. In 1632 the army stormed into the palace and executed 16 high officials, plus the grand vizier, and afterwards soldiers rampaged the streets of Constantinople (modern-day Istanbul), the capital of the Ottoman Empire.

MURAD TAKES CHARGE

Murad was now old enough to rule by himself, and he was pretty furious. He began by executing the soldiers responsible for the executions. Then he banned tobacco and closed coffee houses and wine shops, where plotting might have taken place. Anyone caught plotting against his rule, or suspected of it, was executed. His methods were brutal, but Murad restored law and order and discipline in the army, and the Sultan was the supreme leader again.

BASHING BAGHDAD

Earlier in Murad's reign, while he was still a child, the city of Baghdad had been lost. In 1638 Murad set out to win it back, leading the army himself and fighting alongside his soldiers. He was famous for his physical strength – it was said he could wrestle several opponents at once and defeat the lot, and his favourite weapons were a two-handed broadsword weighing 50 kilograms, and a 60-kilogram mace. Wielding his enormous weapons, he besieged Baghdad for 40 days, and the city was conquered after a bloody massacre. Murad ended up controlling the land surrounding the city as well.

DRANK TO DEATH

Murad died in 1640, when he was only 27, probably because he drank too much alcohol. His mentally ill brother Ibrahim took over as Sultan after his death, and the Ottoman Empire continued for almost another 300 years.

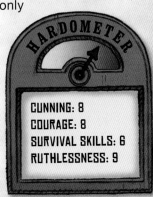

HARDOMETER

CUNNING: 8
COURAGE: 8
SURVIVAL SKILLS: 6
RUTHLESSNESS: 9

NADIR SHAH

Nadir Shah was born a peasant but became an Iranian ruler, created an empire and founded a dynasty.

HARD NUT
RATING: 7

REBEL ARMY

Nadir was born into a Turkish tribe in 1688, part of the Safavid Empire, which included Iran and parts of Turkey and Georgia. He became a soldier for a local chieftain, then formed his own rebel army. In 1726, he led 5,000 of his followers in support of the Safavid shah, Tahmasp II, who had lost the throne of Iran to an Afghan enemy. Nadir's army completely battered the Afghans, and Tahmasp regained the throne.

NADIR ON THE RAMPAGE

Nadir wasn't very impressed with Tahmasp, and replaced him with Tahmasp's young son, while Nadir ruled for him. He modelled himself on Genghis Khan, the rampaging Mongol conqueror of the 1100s. After a couple of years, Nadir had won back lost territories, and started expanding the empire. His army could cover huge distances with amazing speed, and attacked just as fast, taking everyone by surprise.

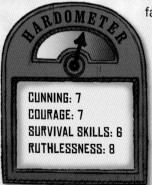

HARDOMETER

CUNNING: 7
COURAGE: 7
SURVIVAL SKILLS: 6
RUTHLESSNESS: 8

INVADING INDIA

In 1736 Nadir put himself on the throne then had the young shah and his family put to death. In 1738, he invaded India, marched on Delhi, killed 30,000 citizens, and stole treasure including the famous Koh-i Noor diamond.

NADIR NOBBLED

Nadir was a brilliant soldier, but not so good at running his newly conquered empire. He made the people of Iran pay enormous taxes, and almost ruined the economy and eventually people started to revolt against him. After an assassination attempt, he started to behave very strangely. He had his own son blinded for allegedly plotting against him, then executed anyone who'd seen the punishment. Eventually his commanders came to finish him off while he slept, but not without a fight: two of them were killed before Nadir was murdered.

ELIZABETH I

Elizabeth was a strong English queen who battled the Spanish Armada and ruled for 45 years.

HARD NUT RATING: 7.3

A DIFFICULT START

Elizabeth was the daughter of Henry VIII and Anne Boleyn, and was only two years old when her mother's head was chopped off on the orders of her father. She wasn't expected to become queen, since she had an older half-brother and half-sister. When her half-brother, Edward VI, died aged 15, Elizabeth's half-sister, Mary, became queen. During Mary's reign, Elizabeth was accused of being part of a rebellion and imprisoned in the Tower of London. She was released when Philip II of Spain, Mary's husband, realised that his wife was making herself even more unpopular by keeping Elizabeth in prison. In 1558 Queen Mary I died without having any children, so Elizabeth became queen.

TROUBLE WITH MARY

Queen Mary had been a Catholic, and didn't like Protestants one little bit – she had hundreds of them burned at the stake. Elizabeth wanted a Protestant England after her sister's reign, but didn't burn any Catholics. But there were Catholic plots against her, one of them possibly involving Elizabeth's cousin, Mary Queen of Scots, who also had a claim to the English throne. Elizabeth kept Mary in prison for 19 years, then, convinced she was plotting against her, had her executed.

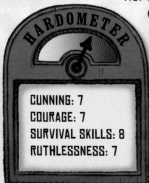

HARDOMETER

CUNNING: 7
COURAGE: 7
SURVIVAL SKILLS: 8
RUTHLESSNESS: 7

SAVED BY THE BEAUTIFUL BRITISH WEATHER!

SPANISH INVADERS

As well as Catholic plots, Elizabeth also had to contend with threats of invasion, the most alarming one of all from King Philip II of Spain. Philip had been married to Mary I, and decided he should be King of England, get rid of Queen Elizabeth, and make England a Catholic country again. He sent a Spanish Armada of around 130 ships as an invasion force, but he was thwarted by stormy weather and the English fleet. But the threat of invasion remained, and huge piles of cash were spent on defending England, leaving the country in debt when Elizabeth died.

ELIZABETH BOWS OUT

Elizabeth died aged 70, having reigned for almost 45 years. Despite the expensive wars, she was popular throughout her reign – so much so that the date she became queen remained a public holiday for 200 years.

MORE HARD NUT BRITISH MONARCHS

We've met head-chopping hard nut Henry VIII of England and his equally hard daughter, Queen Elizabeth I (pages 10 and 46). But they weren't the only tough British monarchs . . .

RICHARD I

Also known as: Richard the Lionheart
Reign: 1189-1199
Hard Nut Deeds: Richard joined the Third Crusade, a fight between Christians and Muslims for control of the Holy Land, and in particular the city of Jerusalem in what's now Israel. Although he was a fearsome fighter and won a lot of battles, Richard returned to England without conquering Jerusalem. But he didn't stay long: he was soon off fighting again, this time in France, where he died besieging a French castle.

MARY I

Also known as: Bloody Mary
Reign: 1553-1558
Hard Nut Deeds: Mary's father, Henry VIII, had been a Catholic until he divorced Mary's mother, married someone else and set up his own Church. We can only imagine that Mary was quite upset by this experience. When she became queen, Mary made England a Catholic country again, and got really cross if anyone practised Protestantism – so cross that she burned hundreds of Protestants at the stake.

EDWARD I

Also known as: Edward Longshanks: The Hammer of the Scots
Reign: 1272-1307
Hard Nut Deeds: Conquering Wales, which he managed after a series of bloody battles. He built forts and castles and installed English nobles in them to keep the Welsh under control, and made his son Prince of Wales. Then he turned his attention to Scotland, where he wasn't so successful, but caused a lot of battles and bloodshed. When he finally defeated Scottish rebel William Wallace he executed him and had bits of him put on display all over Britain.

EDWARD I

SULEIMAN THE MAGNIFICENT

Suleiman the Magnificent was one of the greatest sultans of the mighty Ottoman Empire.

OTTOMAN SULTAN

Suleiman became Sultan of the Ottoman Empire in 1520. When his father died, it's likely that Suleiman's brothers, and his uncles on his father's side, were all killed, so that Suleiman wouldn't have any rivals. The empire he inherited was huge: Suleiman's father, Selim I, had made it triple in size while he was Sultan, and it included Turkey, Greece, Egypt, Syria, some of North Africa and more. Suleiman was now one of the richest rulers in the world. But he had his own plans for expansion.

EXPANDING THE EMPIRE

Suleiman's conquests began in 1521, and continued until he died 45 years later. He rampaged across Europe, Asia and Africa, conquering what's now Iraq from the Safavid Empire, rampaging as far west as Vienna, and sailing across the Mediterranean to capture all the major ports of North Africa, as well as the coasts of Italy and Dalmatia (which is now part of Croatia). The Ottoman fleet ruled the sea, commanded by Suleiman's terrifying Grand Admiral, Barbarossa.

HARDOMETER

CUNNING: 7
COURAGE: 7
SURVIVAL SKILLS: 8
RUTHLESSNESS: 6

GOLDEN AGE

With the riches from conquered lands, Suleiman built impressive and expensive public buildings. The empire grew even richer, and arts such as painting, ceramics and calligraphy flourished. Suleiman's reign became known as a golden age.

SULEIMAN'S LAST BATTLE

In 1566, when he was 72, Suleiman was on his way to Vienna, planning to make it part of the Ottoman Empire as well. He stopped at a castle in Szigetvar, Hungary, with up to about 100,000 troops. But the castle's commander and his troops of only about 2,300 men put up a valiant fight. The castle's commander died as the castle was finally lost to the Ottomans. Suleiman died in his tent – maybe of old age, or maybe from outrage that such a small force had cost him so many lives. But by that time he had an absolutely huge empire that included vast chunks of Europe, Africa, Asia and the Middle East.

WU ZETIAN

Wu Zetian was a clever, ruthless woman who became the one and only Empress of China.

HARD NUT
RATING: 8.5

CONCUBINE

When Wu Zetian (also known as Wu Hou) was 14, in 638 AD, she was sent to Emperor Taizong, second Emperor of the Tang Dynasty. Emperors usually had one wife and lots of concubines, who were like second-class wives, and Wu Zetian became one of them. When the emperor died, Wu Zetian went to live in a Buddhist convent, along with the emperor's other concubines who didn't have children.

JEALOUS EMPRESS

Wu Zetian didn't stay in the convent for long: she was called back to the palace by the new Emperor's wife, Empress Wang, who was jealous of one of the Emperor's concubines, Consort Xiao, and hoped that having Wu Zetian around might help. It didn't. Wu Zetian became Emperor Gaozong's favourite concubine instead, and that gave her power. She accused Empress Wang and Consort Xiao of witchcraft, and they were arrested and then executed.

EMPRESS WU

Emperor Gaozong married Wu Zetian, making her Empress Wu. Any court officials who didn't support her – and there were quite a few – were either sent into exile or executed. Wu Zetian also made sure her own son was named as Gaozong's heir. Emperor Gaozong became sick, and wasn't well enough to rule China, so Wu Zetian ruled for him for the last 23 years of his life. She ruled ruthlessly, crushing opponents and rebellions. She also found time to send troops to invade and conquer Korea.

EVICTING EMPERORS

Wu Zetian ruled for Gaozong until he died in 683 AD and her son became emperor, but Wu Zetian was the real power behind the throne. When her son disagreed with her, she sent him into exile and made a different son emperor instead. Finally, she got rid of the second son as well, and took the throne herself. She ruled on her own from 690 to 705 AD, when she was old and sick, and a group of her enemies saw their chance: they executed Wu Zetian's friends and made her hand over power to one of her sons. She died in 710 AD, the only woman ever to become Empress of China.

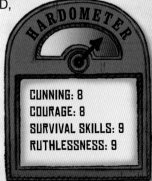

HARDOMETER

CUNNING: 8
COURAGE: 8
SURVIVAL SKILLS: 9
RUTHLESSNESS: 9

NEBUCHADNEZZAR II

King Nebuchadnezzar II was an ancient warrior King of Babylon, who made his empire bigger and more impressive than it had ever been.

HARD NUT RATING: 7

NABOPOLASSAR AND NEBUCHADNEZZAR

Nebuchadnezzar was the son of the Babylonian King Nabopolassar, who defeated the Assyrian Empire (with a bit of help from his friends the Medes, Persians, Scythians and Cimmerians), and completely battered the Assyrian capital Nineveh. Now that Babylon was independent again, Nabopolassar sent Nebuchadnezzar to make Babylon even bigger, by bashing the Egyptian and Assyrian Army at the Battle of Carchemish. Nebuchadnezzar won, and the Babylonian Empire got bigger as a result.

KING NEBUCHADNEZZAR

When Nebuchadnezzar became king in 605 BC, he was set on a path of destruction of his own, and conquered the Cimmerians and Scythians (even though they'd helped his father defeat the Assyrian Empire). Instead of conquering the Median Empire, Nebuchadnezzar married the King of Media's daughter. But he was kept busy crushing rebellions, invading Egypt, and capturing Jerusalem.

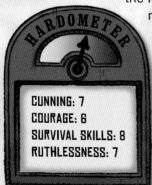

CUNNING: 7
COURAGE: 6
SURVIVAL SKILLS: 8
RUTHLESSNESS: 7

CONQUERING

When you're a power-hungry Babylonian warrior king, there's not much time for putting your feet up. There was a rebellion in

Jerusalem ten years after Nebuchadnezzar had captured it, and he ended up destroying the city and making lots of its citizens leave. After that, it was time for more conquering: he laid siege to the city of Tyre in Phoenicia – 13 long years later the Phoenicians finally accepted the Babylonians as their overlords. Then it was back to Egypt for another attack.

BUILDING

After all that, Nebuchadnezzar went back to Babylon – but not for a rest. Babylon had been laid to ruins during years of war and rebellions. Nebuchadnezzar restored old temples and other buildings to their former glory, and built new ones, as well as new city walls and gates, and an impressive stone bridge and underground passage across the Euphrates River. Most famous of all, though there's a chance it might not have been built by Nebuchadnezzar, were the Hanging Gardens of Babylon, one of the Seven Wonders of the Ancient World.

REIGN OVER

No doubt worn out by all that conquering and building, Nebuchadnezzar died in 562 BC, having ruled Babylon for 43 years.

QUEEN TAMAR OF GEORGIA

Queen Tamar was Georgia's first ever female ruler. She had plans for expansion, and made Georgia the biggest it had ever been.

TROUBLE WITH THE TOFFS

Tamar was born in 1166, the daughter of King George III of Georgia. George named Tamar as his co-ruler, and when he died when Tamar was 18, she became the sole ruler, and Georgia's first ruling queen. Some of the nobles didn't think she should be running Georgia and pushed her around at first. They got her to marry Prince Yuri, who was a good soldier but pretty rubbish otherwise. Queen Tamar quickly toughened up, put her own supporters in power, and stood up to them. She divorced Yuri and sent him into exile, then found a much better husband, David Soslan, who turned out to be a good soldier too.

EXPANSION PLANS

Now that Tamar was properly in power, she started thinking about expanding Georgia. Abu Bakr of Azerbaijan (which was ruled by Turkey) tried to stop her, but Tamar's army, led by her husband David Soslan, defeated him. And Tamar's army didn't stop there: soon it had conquered enormous great chunks of Armenia, mainly by invading areas ruled by Turkish and Persian tribes.

BATTLE OF BASIAN

Suleiman II, Sultan of Rum, tried to put a stop to the Georgian advance. He camped at Basian (now in northeast Turkey) and sent a strongly-worded message demanding that Tamar surrender to him, and also convert to Islam. If she refused she would become one of his concubines. The nobleman who read the message was outraged and Tamar sent a curt reply, then she gave a rousing speech to her troops, and they battered Suleiman II.

GORGEOUS GEORGIAN EMPIRE

By the end of her reign in 1213, Tamar ruled over an empire at the height of its power. Georgia now stretched from the Black Sea in the west, where she established the Trebizond Empire, to the Caspian Sea in the east, and had gained more land to the north and much more to the south. As well as lots of conquering, Tamar had done a lot of praying, and after her death she was made a Christian saint.

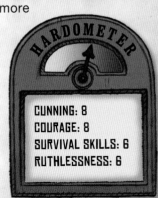

CUNNING: 8
COURAGE: 8
SURVIVAL SKILLS: 6
RUTHLESSNESS: 6

HARD NUT KINGS AND QUEENS TIMELINE

C. 1485 BC

Hatshepsut became the first female Egyptian pharaoh, ruling alongside her stepson.

883 BC

Ashurnasirpal II became King of Assyria, and went on to do lots of conquering.

605 BC

Nebuchadnezzar II became King of Babylon, expanded his empire, and (probably) built one of the Seven Wonders of the World.

480 BC

Queen Artemisia of Halicarnassus commanded ships for the Persians in the Battle of Salamis.

340 BC

Chandragupta, hard nut founder of the Indian Mauryan Empire, was born.

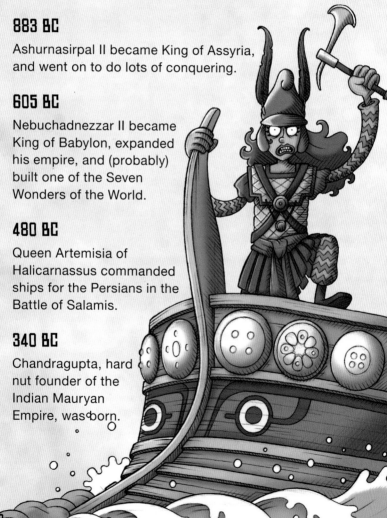

274 AD

Queen Zenobia of Palmyra, who conquered bits of the Roman Empire, was defeated and captured by the Romans.

690 AD

Wu Zetian became sole ruler of China, the only woman in history to become Empress of China.

1015

The fierce Viking warrior king, Harald Hardrada, was born. He was defeated by English King Harold at the Battle of Stamford Bridge.

1213

Queen Tamar died, having conquered a large empire for Georgia. She was later made a Christian saint.

1492

A busy year for King Ferdinand and Queen Isabella of Spain, who defeated the Moors and united Spain, and funded Christopher Columbus's expedition to the New World.

1502

Montezuma became the last ever Emperor of the Aztecs, defeated by the invading Spanish.

1509

Eighteen-year-old Henry VIII became King of England, and went on to do lots of marrying and head-chopping.

1520

Suleiman the Magnificent became Sultan of a huge Ottoman Empire, and began a path of conquest to make it absolutely huge.

1558

Armada-battling Elizabeth I became Queen of England.

1623

Murad IV became Sultan of the mighty Ottoman Empire, and made it even bigger and more powerful than before.

1624

Nzinga Mbande became Queen of the Ndongo in western Africa.

1688

Nadir Shah was born a peasant, but ended up ruling an Iranian Empire.

1740

Conquering monarch Frederick the Great became King of Prussia, which he had doubled in size by the time he died.

C. 1787

Ferocious Zulu King Shaka was born around this date.

1810

Hard nut Hawaiian King Kamehameha became ruler of all the Hawaiian Islands, after bashing or persuading everyone into submission.

GLOSSARY

ASSASSINATED Killed for political reasons

BESIEGED Surrounded by enemy forces

CALLIGRAPHY Decorative handwriting or lettering

CHIEFTAIN Powerful leader of a group of people

CIVIL WAR War between groups of people from the same country or state

CONCUBINE A woman who lives with and is in a relationship with a man who is not his official wife and has a lower status than his wife

CURT Rude and brief when speaking

DIVORCE When a marriage is ended by law

DYNASTY A series of rulers from the same family

EMPIRE A group of states or countries ruled by one leader or state

EXILE Banned from your native country

INSCRIPTION Something written on or cut into a surface

INTERROGATED Questioned thoroughly and forcefully

MACE A heavy club with a spiked metal head

MARAUDING Going about in search of things to steal or people to attack

MASSACRE Brutally kill

MUSKET A gun with a long barrel

PHARAOHS Leaders of Ancient Egypt

PLOTTING Secretly making plans to carry something out

PROTESTANTS A group of Christians formed in reaction to the problems they saw in the Catholic Church

PROVINCE Region of land that belongs to a country or empire

RAMMED Roughly crushed or forced

RAMPAGING Behaving in a violent or angry way

REVOLT Rebel

RUTHLESS Showing no pity or kindness to others

SHAH Monarch of Iran

SULTAN A Muslim king

TACTICS Plans or systems

ULCERS Open sores on the body

INDEX